SR-71 BLACKBIRD

To BROTHER Jim—

WiTH ADMiRATION AND AFFecTION
ALWAYS!

Bob

3-9-94

Lockheed's Mach 3 Hot Shot

Osprey Colour Series

SR-71 BLACKBIRD

PAUL F CRICKMORE

First published in summer 1987 by Osprey
Publishing Limited,
59 Grosvenor Street, London W1X 9DA

Reprinted winter 1988 and autumn 1989

British Library Cataloguing in Publication Data

Crickmore, Paul F.
    SR-71 Blackbird; Lockheed's Mach 3 hot shot —
    (Osprey Colour Series)
    1. SR-71 (Jet reconnaissance plane) —
    Pictorial works
    I. Title
    623.74'67   UG242.R4

ISBN 0-85045-794-7

Editor Dennis Baldry
Designed by David Tarbutt
Printed in Hong Kong

Front cover An SR-71A Blackbird from Det 4
manoeuvres for the benefit of Chris Allan's
camera near its base at RAF Mildenhall in
Suffolk, England, in the summer of 1986
(*courtesy Chris Allan Aviation Library*)

Back cover Crewed by Majors Jim Jiggens
(pilot) and RSO Ted Ross, SR-71A serial
64-17964, callsign SHEIK 99, launches from
Mildenhall in February 1987. The aircraft was
forced to abort its mission $1\frac{1}{2}$ hours later after
experiencing bypass door problems

Right At the invitation of Det 4's commander,
Lieutenant Colonel Nevin Cunningham, author
Paul Crickmore experiences 'the bag' by
wearing a David Clark S1030 pressure suit
used by SR-71 crews.

To Clarence L 'Kelly' Johnson

First flown from Palmdale, California, on 22 December 1964 by Lockheed experimental test pilot Robert J Gilliland, the SR-71 strategic reconnaissance aircraft has captured the imagination of aviation professionals and enthusiasts alike since the existence of 'Senior Crown' — Strategic Air Command's codename for the SR-71 programme — was revealed by an electioneering President Lyndon B Johnson on 25 July of that same year.

Designed to cruise in afterburner at Mach 3 (about 2100 mph), the SR-71 operates at altitudes in the region of 85,000 ft. Despite ambient air temperatures averaging minus 60 degrees Centigrade, the SR-71 is far from frozen at its cruising altitude. At high Mach cruise, thermodynamic heating (skin friction) generates airframe temperatures in excess of 200 degrees Centigrade, a condition described by A-12 experimental test pilot Lou Schalk as 'a thermal thicket'. Both crewmen are equipped with a space suit to protect them from the hazardous effects of decompression, embullism, hypoxia, and cold. Their S1030 'gold suits' also provide the necessary life-support in the event of cockpit decompression or ejection at extreme altitudes.

The aircrew recruited into Senior Crown are unquestionably some of the most competent and highly-motivated fliers in the US Air Force. Project insiders and 'crew dogs' (pilot and RSO) have long referred to the SR-71 as the 'Habu', a nickname given to it by the Japanese when the aircraft was first deployed to Kadena Air Base on Okinawa in 1968. The aircraft seemed to resemble the poisonous pit viper resident on the Ryuku islands.

SR-71 BLACKBIRD — LOCKHEED'S Mach 3 Hot Shot is a follow-up to the author's hugely successful *LOCKHEED SR-71 BLACKBIRD* (ISBN 0-85045-653-3) in the Osprey Air Combat series, first published in October 1986. If you would like to know the full story of the SR-71 and its predecessors this author's 200-page Air Combat volume, illustrated with over 160 black and white photographs and 12 photographs in full colour, is without doubt the standard work on the subject.

This Colour Series book would not have been possible without the cooperation of Lieutenant Colonel Nevin Cunningham and the following US Air Force personnel: Colonel Dave Pinsky, Lieutenant Colonel Joe Kinego, Lieutenant Colonel Frank Stampf, Captain Joe Saxon, Lieutenant June Green, Sargeants Dan D'Antonio and Ted Rekowski. The author would also like to thank the Habu and tanker crews for their help and hospitality, Dennis Baldry, Don and Anita Jensen, Chris Palmer, and Jane Harvey of Canon (UK) Limited.

The photographs in this book were taken by the author at Beale AFB, Kadena AB, and RAF Mildenhall between October 1986 and February 1987. Canon camera equipment was used throughout, loaded with Kodachrome 64 and Ektachrome 200 film.

Contents

Habu training mission

Left SR-71A, callsign ASPEN 31, drops back from the KC-135Q tanker after a successful air refuelling (AR) contact

The same aircraft moves purposefully to the hammerhead for engine trim checks prior to launch from Beale AFB, California. ASPEN callsigns are used for all stateside SR-71 training sorties; the two-seat SR-71B pilot trainer always uses the callsign ASPEN 39, while 'A' model flights start with the number 30 and then run consecutively throughout the day

Left Habu pilot Major Tom Danielson makes for his seat inside the Physiological Support Division (PSD) van which will transport him and RSO Major Stan Gudmandson to their aircraft

To prevent the 'crew dogs' from sweating buckets under the hot California sun, their $30,000 S1030 pressure suits are connected to the van's in-built suit ventilation system

Between layers of thin cirro-stratus cloud, ASPEN 31 slides in behind the tanker for its initial AR shortly after takeoff. In poor visibility, particularly during a radio-silent operational mission, the '135 will sometimes dump fuel through the boom to help the Habu's crew spot the tanker

ASPEN 31 stabilized in the pre-contact position behind the tanker before moving in to hook-up on the boom. The SR-71 is fitted with a Tacan (tactical air navigation) aid to enable the crew to accurately measure the distance and bearing to the tanker for a trouble-free RV (rendezvous)

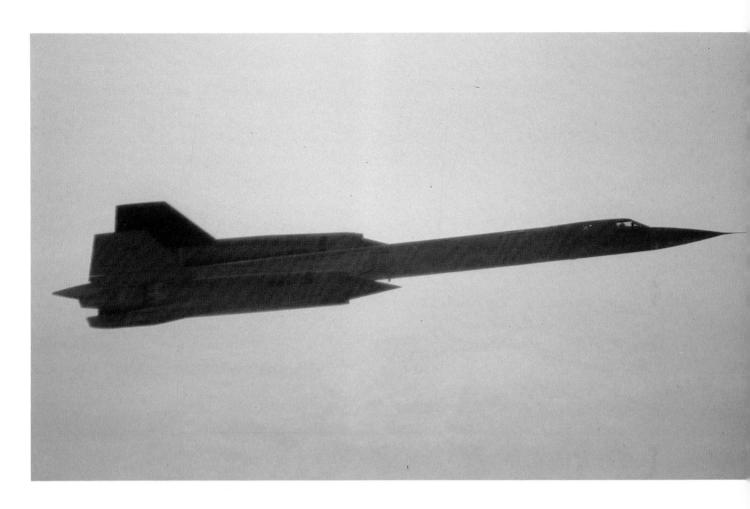

Topped-off with fuel, the 'Lady in Black'
commences her acceleration and climb

Airborne in KC-135Q BLOWN 73 (serial 59-1490) aircraft commander Captain Phil Swanson and Lieutenant Dave Boardman (right of picture) check the aircraft's fuel specifics en route to the initial point (IP) for the refuelling operation

Left The senior tanker navigator checks the '135's ground track with radar as the aircraft maintains 350 knots at flight level 260 (26,000 ft)

Captain Bonner, the other navigator aboard BLOWN 73, verifies the tanker's arrival at the second air refuelling contact point (ARCP).

Overleaf Pilot Tom Danielson hooks up to BLOWN 73; on contact (right-hand picture) the tanker's copilot activates the booster pumps which send JP-7 fuel cascading into the SR-71 at the rate of 5500 lb/min

Tom Danielson gets plugged off with 55,000 lb of fuel by the 'boomer' (boom operator) in tanker lead BLOWN 72 over the Rockies during his second AR of the day. The tanker and receiver can communicate with one another by a ship-to-ship radio link installed in the boom which is activated when the nozzle makes contact with the SR-71's refuelling receptacle. **Right** The reconnaissance systems officer (RSO) in back has just two small windows and a ventral viewscope to catch a glimpse of the outside world. Visibility from the front cockpit is obviously much better, but the restricted view upwards is self-evident

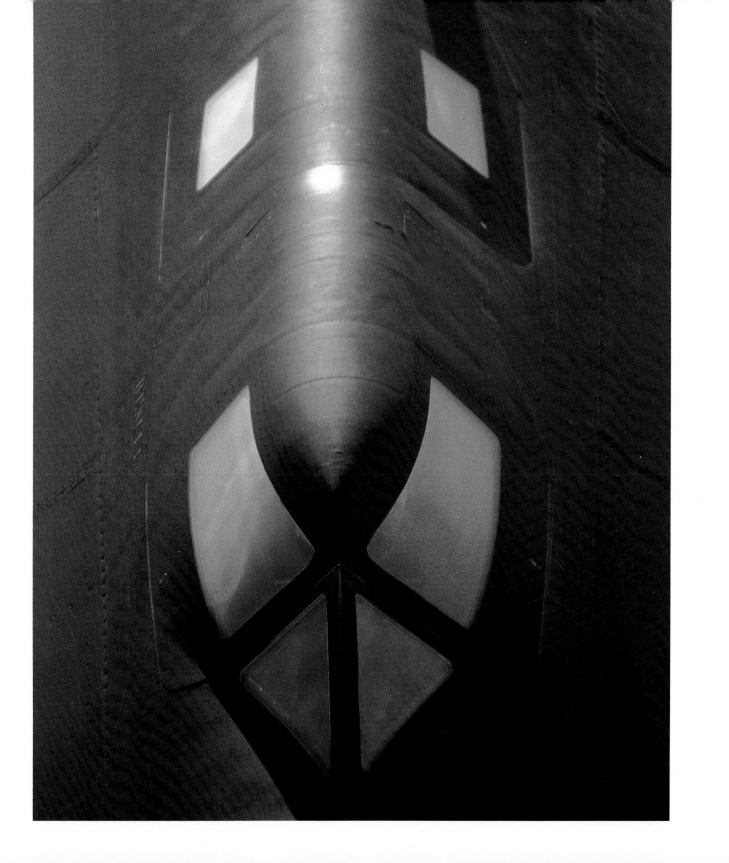

Left Full to capacity, ASPEN 31 streams fuel from innumerable tiny leaks. These disappear by the time the aircraft reaches cruise speed (Mach 3.2, 2112 mph) and warms up several hundred degrees' Centigrade

Above With the final AR completed, Tom Danielson clears the tanker before accelerating away for the final portion of his sortie with RSO Stan Gudmandson

Overleaf Billowing its 40-ft diameter brake 'chute, ASPEN 31 returns to Beale after a successful 2½-hour training flight

Silver Sows

Left As any SR-71 'crew dog' will confirm, it's a case of 'no tankers, no go'. Boeing's indefatigable KC-135Q (occasionally referred to as the 'Silver Sow', because it suckles receivers and handles like a pig) is a vital part of any SR-71 mission. This example is beginning its let-down into Beale towards the setting sun

Chocks at the ready, a maintenance crew stands by to park the returning KC-135Q from which this picture was taken

27

The 349th and 350th Air Refueling Squadrons are dedicated to SR-71 operations and they are an integral part of the 9th Strategic Reconnaissance Wing (SRW). Their tankers sport four Maltese crosses on a yellow fin band

All angles and dangles, KC-135Q serial 59-1520
lines up for a landing

U.S. AIR
0112
STRATOSAURUS
C/C SSGT F. LUNGA
A/C/C SRA D. PORTER
TOW BAR LIMIT

The crew of *Stratosaurus*, serial 58-0112, callsign PROSE 87, begin to emerge after a training flight, which included several touch-and-go or 'crash and dash' landings. **Above** In the crew bus en route to the maintenance debrief, Major Ron Forest and his crew reflect on their performance during the mission

Refuelling a KC-135Q is accomplished from one of the underground storage tanks at Beale

A tanker being loaded for the long flight from
California to Suffolk, England. KC-135Q serial
58-0099 will remain in the UK for a stint of TDY
(temporary duty) to support SR-71 operations from
Detachment 4 of the 9th SRW at RAF Mildenhall

Left Security police dog Homa (not to be confused with a crew dog) and his handler, Airman 1st Class Edwards, check 58-0099 for non-standard items before departure

Above In common with the standard KC-135A, the 'Q' model is equipped with a High Speed Boom under the rear fuselage

When 58-0099 touched down at RAF Mildenhall, this tanker was ready to return to California.

The departure of a heavily laden J57-engined '135 or GLOB (ground loving old bastard) is always a noisy, smokey affair

58-0088, callsign HERO 93, is swallowed up by mist as it gets airborne from Mildenhall at 0920 hr on 8 January 1987

Five-and-a-half hours later, 58-0062, callsign
HERO 94, recovers in late afternoon sunshine.
HERO 94 was the fourth of four tankers launched
in support of SR-71 YALE 16 on this particular day

These pages Kadena Air Base, Okinawa: 58-0103 exits the active runway and taxies to the parking area after flying in support of an operational SR-71 mission

Overleaf Although the 349th and 350th AREFSs fly California-based training sorties and deploy six KC-135Qs to Kadena and a further six to Mildenhall, the tanker ramp at Beale is still awash with many tails. **Inset** To boost thrust on takeoff, J57-powered '135s use water and alcohol augmentation. Power is increased by a total of 44 per cent by injecting 670 US gal of warm water (which lasts 125 seconds) into the engine combustion chambers

Beale's best

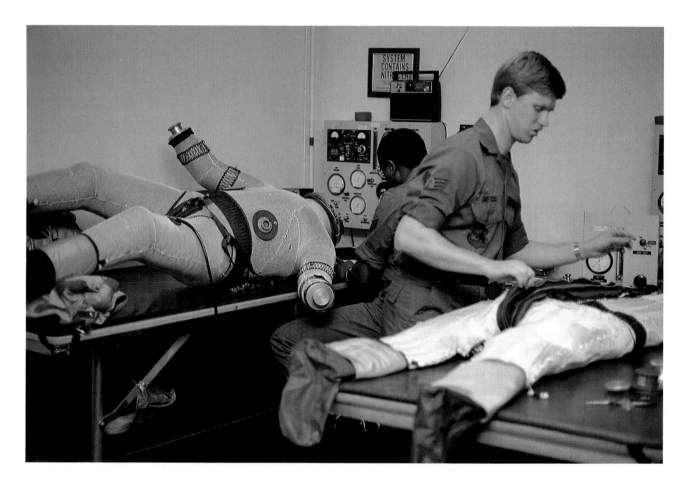

Left A macabre line up of S1030 pressure suits, standard issue for SR-71, TR-1, and U-2 crews. Identical suits were worn by NASA Astronauts for the first four Space Shuttle missions. **Above** After every 150 flight hours the pressure suits receive a complete service. The suit in the background is inflated to check the inner (bladder) layer for leaks

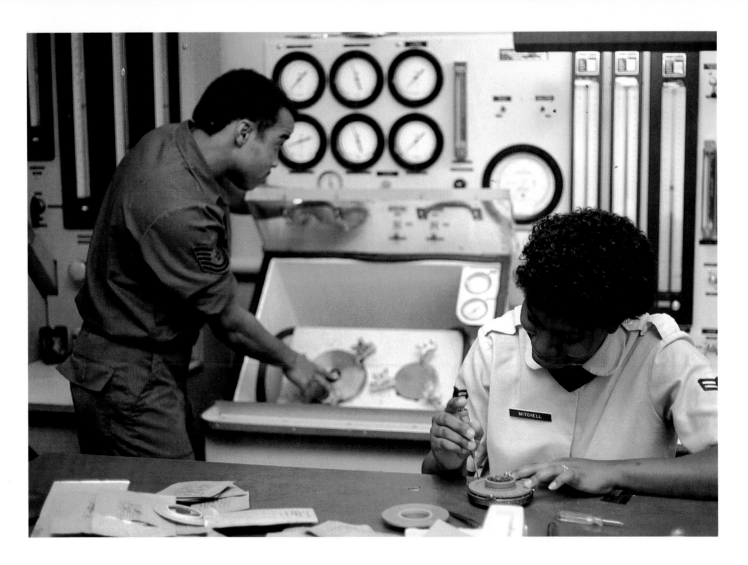

The valves in the pressure suit are removed,
serviced, and tested under pressure

Before a mission, SR-71 crew dogs receive a high protein, low residue meal of steak and eggs — the Pepsi is optional

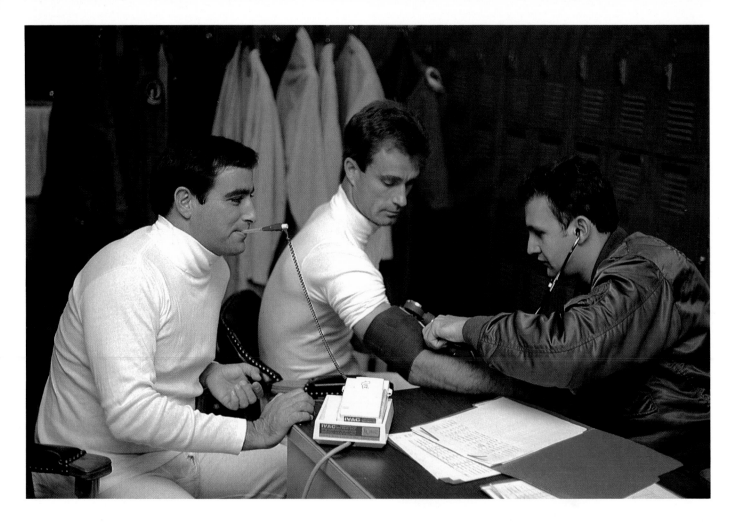

After the meal comes a brief medical examination. Major Duane Noll and his RSO, Major Tom Veltri, (left) have their blood pressure and temperature checked

With all systems go, Duane and Tom taxi out in
SR-71A serial 64-17975 for a 'Moby Dick' training
sortie off the California coast

Overleaf Watched by the groundcrew, pilot Duane
Noll advances the throttles one at a time to fine
tune the engines during the Pre-Takeoff Check

Left With one engine operating at maximum dry thrust (ie, without afterburner), the SR-71 squats nose low, compressing the nose gear leg. **Above** Two groundcrew crouch next to the main gears, ready to pull the chocks from the wheels. The senior crew chief up front ensures that all safety pins and static tags are removed before flight

At precisely 1600 hr SR-71A serial 64-17975, callsign ASPEN 30, launches from Beale, pursued by a pair of crackling shock-studded 'tiger tails'. Rapid gear retraction ensures that the 300-knot extension limit is not exceeded

ASPEN 30 manoeuvres away from the tanker after being refuelled. Interestingly, because of the speed envelope limits of the tanker it is often necessary (especially in warmer climes) for the SR-71 pilot to engage 'min burner' on *one* engine to maintain contact on the tanker (flat out at 350 knots at 26,000 ft) as the last 10,000 lb of fuel is delivered. This added thrust in needed to compensate for the additional aerodynamic drag generated by the SR-71 as it approaches maximum weight. The speed limit problem will cease to exist when the KC-135Qs are finally retrofitted with CFM56 engines, since the tanker will then be able to fly 25 knots faster during the hook-up

Virtually all SR-71 sorties from Beale are crew training flights. It is therefore not uncommon to see a Habu bashing around the traffic pattern performing practice instrument and landing approaches

An experienced SR-71 pilot feeds in some right boot on the rudder pedals as he sets up an asymmetric approach, simulating a power failure on the left engine

Originally employed by the 9th SRW as a companion trainer for SR-71 crews, the Northrop T-38A Talon is also used by U-2 and KC-135Q pilots to give them more flight experience. The relatively low operating cost of the T-38 means that high sortie rates can be generated. 1st Lieutenant Scott Wilhelm and his instructor, Captain Ralph Demeritt, practice a no-flap approach in 60-0578

Same aircraft, same crew, full flap approach

T-38 serial 64-13212 flares for a fast, no flap
SR-71-like touchdown

White Shark, serial 60-0581, tucks away the gear
and heads for the wild blue. An extremely popular
aircraft, the T-38 became operational with the US
Air Force in March 1961. **Overleaf** Yet another
sortie chalked up as *White Shark* awaits wheel
chocks

NTE SHARK

C SRA SHANK

U.S. AIR FORCE T-38A NO-
A.F. SERIAL NO. 00-0501

SERVICE THIS AIRCRAFT WITH GRADE
JP-4 FUEL. IF NOT AVAILABLE, T.O. NO.
42B1-1-14 WILL BE CONSULTED FOR
EMERGENCY ACTION.

SUITABLE FOR USE OF AROMATIC FUEL

1. PUSH LATCH TO C
2. PULL "D" HANDLE
   TO JETTISON CAN

WARNING
THIS AIRPLANE CONTAINS A
CANOPY REMOVER CONTAINING
AN EXPLOSIVE CHARGE. SEE APPLICABLE
-2 AIRCRAFT T.O. FOR COMPLETE
INSTRUCTIONS

U.S. AIRF

STEP

STEP

PORT

Left Back on the ground after an hour of 'fun in the sun'. The T-38 has a maximum speed of Mach 1.3 (860 mph) at altitude

Above *White Shark* basks in strong California sunshine before the next sortie. The airbrakes are extended

Overleaf T-38s stand ready on the ramp with *Wind Breaker*, serial 64-13297, in foreground. **Inset, left** The T-38 is generally 'user friendly' with few maintenance quirks. **Inset, right** Like most fast jets, the T-38 is equipped for single-point pressure refuelling

Above Beale is also home to the U-2. Groundcrew attach 'pogos' to a U-2R before it continues its journey to the ramp after the completion of a low altitude test flight

Left The training of U-2 and SR-71 crews at Beale was formerly conducted by a single strategic reconnaissance training squadron, namely the 4029th SRTS. Today the redesignated 5th SRTS trains pilots for the U-2 programme exclusively. Gear down, a piggy-back Lockheed U-2CT trainer drifts serenely downwind in the traffic pattern

71

A spate of unfortunate accidents early in the U-2
programme emphasized the need to practice
landing techniques, as the aircraft could 'bite'
unless caution was exercised

Lockheed TR-1, serial '1074 of the 99th SRS, flies
a sedate circuit before making a full-stop landing

Habu habitat

Left SR-71A serial 64-17960, callsign TRULY 55, taxies out at Mildenhall piloted by ex-Thunderbirds' demonstration pilot Major Jim Jiggens

Above Lieutenant Colonel Nevin Cunningham, commander of Det 4 at Mildenhall, discusses the results of a trawl for potential SR-71 crews from UK F-111 units with Lieutenant Colonel Joe Kinego, (right) commander of the 1st Strategic Reconnaissance Squadron

Left Pilot Major Brian Shul has his GN-121394 helmet lowered into place

Right With the dressing ritual almost complete, Walt Watson's helmet chin tab is adjusted to prevent his suit from ballooning excessively, and the helmet rising, during an emergency inflation

Below RSO Major Walt Watson is helped into his pressure suit by two PSD specialists. If not the ultimate in 'foundation fashion', Long Johns are certainly the most comfortable. The need for optimum operational efficiency in the high workload environment of an SR-71 cockpit has resulted in a policy of teaming crew members for their entire three to four year tour of duty on the aircraft

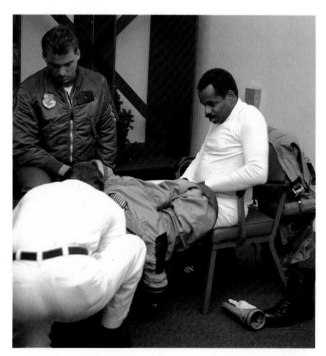

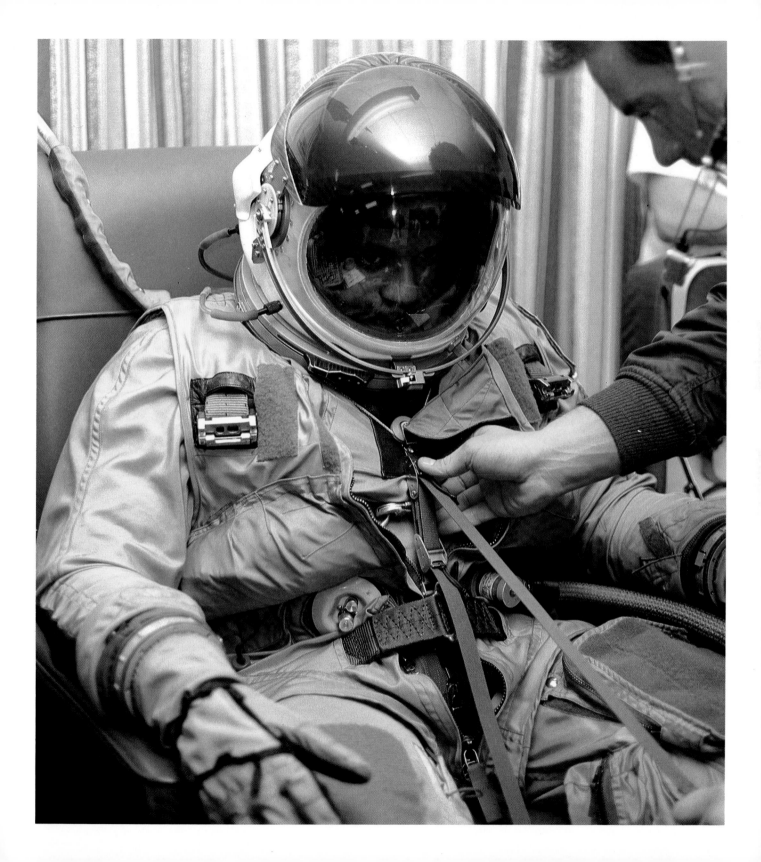

Left Major Jim Jiggens is the senior Standardization/Evaluation (Stan/Eval) pilot on the SR-71. The task of a flight evaluator is to ensure that all crews maintain the highest levels of proficiency

Above Majors Brian Shul and Walt Watson (centre) receive the customary handshake from Major Ted Ross before departing from Mildenhall on an operational mission. The two SR-71 crews detached to Mildenhall alternate between flying and ground duties

Preceding pages Engine start: as the engine is
spooled up to 3200 rpm by compressed air, a
green flash in the combustion chamber indicates
that a shot of Triethylborane (TEB) has done its job
and ignited the left J58. Normal fuel igniters are
unable to generate the required temperatures so a
chemical process is therefore used. Its flash
resistant JP-7 fuel protects the SR-71 from the
threat of inadvertant ignition as a result of the
combination of high airframe and fuel temperatures
during the hot portion of flight at high speed cruise

Above Operation of the SR-71 requires many
items of unique ground equipment. The cart on the
left provides cooling air to the avionics bays, while
the unit on the right is used to program the
aircraft's astro-inertial navigation system (AINS)

The first of several control system checks is carried out in the barn. Movement of the vertical stabilizers is limited in flight to ± 20 degrees below Mach 0.5 and ± 10 degrees above. This control limitation ensures that adequate directional control can be achieved in the event of high speed asymmetic flight

Cockpit canopies are locked and all support systems clear — the groundcrew await the signal to pull chocks

TRULY 55 swings out of the barn and moves
purposefully towards the runway at about 20 mph

TRULY 55 arrives at the hammerhead for Runway 11 at Mildenhall. The other SR-71 flight crew detached to Det 4 have taken up position in the control vehicle (headlights on, in background) to observe the pre-flight engine run-ups

To obtain maximum engine efficiency, the pilot fine
tunes exhaust gas temperature (EGT) before
engaging automatic engine trim

Venting fuel from the boat-tail, TRULY 55 hits the burners. These often light up asymmetrically and the power differential is compensated for by nose-wheel steering (as seen by the rudder deflection) to prevent the aircraft veering off the runway centreline. The low green flash from the right engine indicates TEB ignition in the burner cans lighting the afterburner

The thrust from the Pratt & Whitney J58s is massive. In barely 20 seconds 60 tons of fuel and titanium reaches 215 knots. Standard operating procedure calls for takeoff to be made with either a 50 or 66 per cent fuel load. This ensures that a greater degree of control is maintained in the event of an engine failure on takeoff. Designed by the great Bill Brown, the J58 engine is rated at 32,500 lb of thrust in afterburner at sea level

Major Brian Shul 'rotates' the nose of ANNEX 55 to about 10 degrees Alpha (pitch angle) immediately before unstick

At approximately 230 knots YALE 16 climbs away
from Runway 29 at Mildenhall

Overleaf Gears still retracting, YALE 16 maintains
a pitch angle of 10 degrees as she climbs through
the murk

As YALE 16 scorches her way through a shroud of thin mist, Major Tom Danielson is just seconds away from heaving back on the pole to establish an initial climb rate in excess of 10,000 ft/min. Thanks to the high humidity, the vortical flow from the outer wings is superbly illustrated

SR-71A serial 64-17973 breaks off from a practice
instrument approach to go-around

Left Blackbird beat-up: Major Jim Jiggens in SR-71A serial 64-17960, callsign TRULY 55, 'burns weeds' after returning from an operational mission

Above Mobile Control: an experienced SR-71 crew act as an extra pair of eyes and ears throughout the entire mission. The mobile control crew performs a supervisory role during flight preparation, launch, flight monitoring, recovery, and post-flight phases of the mission. RSO Tom Veltri (standing) and pilot Duane Noll watch a touchdown

Maintaining about 155 knots and 12½ degrees Alpha, Jim Jiggens flares TRULY 55 before touchdown

Brake 'chute deployed, Tom Danielson pins
YALE 16 to the runway. The pilot activates the
three-stage 'chute system by pulling a yellow and
black toggle lever

The 40-ft diameter 'chute deploys rapidly and takes a big bite out of the aircraft's momentum. As the SR-71 slows down on the roll out it's joined on the runway by Mobile Control

Right Brake 'chute doors agape, TRULY 55 taxies back to her barn at Mildenhall. The 'chute is jettisioned at 55 knots to prevent its heavy metal shroud-line clevis from impacting the skin of the rear fuselage

The pilot waits for the crew chief and his wing
walkers to guide the aircraft before progressing
back into the barn

As ANNEX 55 comes to a halt inside the barn technicians place fans adjacent to the main wheels to cool the brakes. **Right** By the time the crew step out of their cockpits the groundcrew is already busy securing the aircraft and replacing safety pins and static tags

Returning from an operational sortie on 10 November 1986, the inlet guide vanes of SR-71A 64-17973 became locked in the cambered position during the transition from high Mach to subsonic flight. After the necessary maintenance was completed this engine test confirmed that the problem had been fixed

With its landing light aglow for the benefit of the camera, Major Brian Shul prepares to taxi 64-17973 back to its barn on completion of the engine run-up

Right Habu keeper: restraint up to and including armed force is authorized to counter unauthorized persons crossing that red line. The guard is armed with a 5.56 mm M16 automatic rifle

Below The Mobile Processing Center (MPC) is located within a fenced compound inside one of Mildenhall's hangars. All of the reconnaissance data collected by the SR-71s deployed to Det 4 is processed and evaluated from within these air transportable cabins

SR-71A serial 64-17967 at Kadena AB after returning in difficult crosswind conditions from a short operational mission on 25 November 1986. The aircraft is crewed by Major Duane Noll and RSO Major Tom Veltri

Habu walk-around

Left A distinctly chilling impersonation of Darth Vader, the evil master of The Force in George Lucas' *Star Wars* movies

Above The nose boom consists of a compensated pitot static probe and an offset hemispherical head flow direction sensor. These provide static and dynamic pressure inputs for the DAFICS, INS, and flight instrumentation

Preceding pages The fuselage forebody accounts for 40 per cent of the SR-71's length, which is 103.8 ft. The majority of the mission sensors are located within the chine, the lateral fuselage extensions

Right Palletized, close-look cameras or sideways looking radar (SLR) units can be fitted inside the chine bays just forward of the wing leading edge. Electronic intelligence (ELINT) is gathered by two recording devices in the bays further forward. Also housed in the chine, the digital automatic flight inlet control system (DAFICS) ensures that the inlet spikes and various bleed air doors are correctly scheduled throughout the flight. Finally, a central airborne performance analyser (CAPA) is also accommodated in the chine. It records the performance of 170 aircraft subsystems to reduce maintenance manhours

114

The 'dents' on either side of the nose boom provide a housing for the radar warning receivers (RWRs). These antennae passively monitor various missile and fighter radars, allowing the RSO to take the appropriate electronic or other measures to counter any interference with the mission

The longitudinal corrugations applied to the wing
surfaces help to minimize the effects of sustained
heat-soak on the structure by alleviating thermal
expansion. After a mission, the brake 'chute doors
remain open (as here) when the aircraft taxies back
after landing

These two views illustrate the 'break line' for the interchangeable nose section. The aircraft at left is equipped with an operational radar nose, while the Beale-based SR-71 shown above has the ballast nose used for training flights. The third option, a panoramic nose fitted with an optical barrel camera (OBC) for horizon-to-horizon photographic coverage, is seldom seen

The inlet spikes regulate the amount of air entering the inlet by moving progressively rearwards as the aircraft's speed increases. **Above and bottom right** The fully forward position which the spike maintains up to Mach 1.25. **Top right** The spike at the limit of its 26-inch aft translation, showing the configuration of the inlet at Mach 3 and above. At this point the capture area has increased by 112 per cent, while the throat diameter at the point of minimum cross-section further down the intake has decreased by 54 per cent in order to hold the tri-sonic shockwave in the correct position. At Mach 2.2 the inlet produces 13 per cent of the overall thrust, the engine and ejector accounting for 73 and 14 per cent respectively. The corresponding figures at maximum cruising speed, Mach 3.2, are inlet 54, engine 17.6, ejector 28.4 per cent

Manufactured by BF Goodrich, the main gear typres are impregnated with aluminium powder to reflect the airframe heat generated thermodynamically at cruising speed. The main gear tyres are inflated to a pressure of 415 psi

Right A titanium shroud is fitted inside each main gear well to help protect the tyres from possible heat damage during sustained Mach 3 flight. The combination of the shroud and tyre impregnation seems to work well because blow outs are extremely rare

Left The SR-71's unusual main gear has a hollow axle arrangement which enables any wheel to be changed without removing the other two

Right Unlike the mains, the nose gear bay is kept cool by the aircraft's environmental air system and therefore no further protection is required for the nose wheel tyres

Left A pair of 105 litre nitrogen dewars are carried in the nose gear bay to pressurize the fuel system and purge the tanks of vapour as fuel is burned off

Above The all-moving tailplane fins are each canted inboard by 15 degrees to reduce the rolling moment due to sideslip and vertical deflection

Overleaf A ribbon brake 'chute lies on Runway 29 at RAF Mildenhall after being jettisioned by an arriving SR-71